Walking Grandma Home

A story of grief, hope, and healing

Written by Nancy Bo Flood

Illustrated by Ellen Shi

ZONDERkidz

Copyright © 2023 by Nancy Bo Flood
Illustrations © 2023 by Zondervan

Requests for information should be addressed to:
Zonderkidz, 3900 Sparks Drive SE, Grand Rapids, Michigan 49546

ISBN 978-0-310-77124-1 (hardcover)
ISBN 978-0-310-77128-9 (ebook)

Zonderkidz is a trademark of Zondervan.

Art direction & design: Diane Mielke

Printed in Thailand

23 24 25 26 27 /IMG/ 10 9 8 7 6 5 4 3 2 1

To Mom and Dad:
throughout the cycles of life and death,
they loved us, all eight of us.

–NBF

Grandma smiled. "Little Lee, I'm going away soon, going home."

Home? I thought. *Grandma is already home.*

That summer all my aunts, uncles, and cousins were in town for Tara's wedding. Grandma asked me to walk with her down the long aisle. I handed Grandma her cane and she held on to my shoulder. My little cousin, Maria, skipped and twirled, tossing rose petals everywhere.

"Thank you for being my helper," Grandma said. We sat together. I held Grandma's cane and didn't drop it once.

That was summer. Now it's winter. Grandma is not the same.

Mom says she had a stroke and the hurt is inside. Even lots of Band-Aids won't help.

Yesterday, everyone began arriving at Grandma's house.

Uncle Tony set down a tray of doughnuts. I took the one with the most frosting. "Will Grandma get better soon?"

Uncle Tony's eyes were watery. He didn't answer.

That doughnut stayed stuck in my throat. My uncle gave me a glass of milk.
"It's Grandma's time to leave us.
She is ready to go home."

"This is her home. I don't want Grandma to leave." I looked up at Uncle Tony and frowned.

"I know, Lee, but Grandma will have no more pain, in a special place some people call heaven." Uncle Tony sat down so we were face to face, swallowed a few times, and then took a catchy kind of breath. "Today, we are all here to say good-bye. Grandma is dying."

Then all of me felt quiet and sad.

"I don't want to say that kind of good-bye," I whispered. "I'm Grandma's helper. I walk her to the window to watch the birds. We drink tea in fancy cups with red roses painted all around the edges. Even if it's way past bedtime, we sit outside on the porch.

Grandma wraps her shawl around us and tells me stories about when she was a little girl and took care of all the chickens and one mean rooster."
"Rooster and chicken stories?" Uncle Tony chuckled.

I smiled back at my uncle. "That rooster is why Grandma has a missing tooth in front. He chased her out of the chicken coop. She tripped and *splat!* Landed on her apron full of eggs and knocked her tooth clean out. That rooster ate it! Grandma's mom said, 'We will have that rooster for dinner.' And they did."

We both laughed. "Lee, you will be our new storyteller. Grandma would like that."

Then I remembered. Grandma's shawl! I found it on the porch swing and hurried back inside. "This will help Grandma if she's a little bit scared."

I looked toward Grandma's room.
"Are Mom and Dad in there?"

Uncle Tony nodded and gave me a little hug. "We're all a little scared about saying good-bye, but we can help each other. And we can let Grandma know that it's okay to leave."

Uncle Tony nodded. I reached for his hand and held on tight.

Mom looked so sad. She helped me spread the shawl over Grandma's shoulders just the way she liked it.

"Would you like to hold Grandma's hand?
She can't talk, but she knows you are here."

"Does dying mean she is hurting?"

"Mostly, Grandma is waiting." Mom put her hand on Grandma's.

"Can I sing the 'over-the-rainbow' song we sing when my knees get skinned-up?"

Mom nodded and sang along. I think Grandma liked it even if some of our words weren't right.

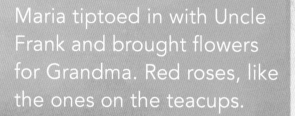

Maria tiptoed in with Uncle Frank and brought flowers for Grandma. Red roses, like the ones on the teacups.

Mom hugged me extra close. "All the people Grandma loves are here, in person or in spirit, walking with her in their hearts." Then everyone was quiet.

I looked around the room, looked at all of us helping each other.
My heart hurt, but I was helping too. Helping walk my grandma home.

Information for Parents, Caregivers, and Counselors

Every child grieves differently. The mood of a child coping with loss may quickly shift, and then behaviors may switch from withdrawn to angry acting-out or being silly. And inside, children often worry, "Who will die next?" Every feeling is real and needs to be listened to, and honored.

Children often don't want to talk about death, but when they do, be ready to listen. Encourage their comments without inserting your own needs. Grief is not a straight line. It's normal for birthdays, family gatherings, holidays, even seasons to stir up feelings that seemed to be "done."

Time together can be an opportunity for sharing and healing. Creating ways to honor the person's memory can be a positive way of grieving. Here are some suggestions:

1. We honor those we love who have died by "talking story." Sometimes we cry when we share our story; sometimes we laugh. Two ways to explore this with a child are:
   • Share a favorite memory. Begin together with "I remember when …" followed by funny moments or special traditions.
   • Create a "memory book" together. Follow the child's lead. Draw pictures. Add photographs. Invite the child to write (or dictate) a few sentences.

2. Make a list of the person's favorites: ice cream, doughnuts, a pet, a song, a baseball team. The child might enjoy creating a poem from this list.

3. Write a letter to the person who has died: Start with "Dear___," and let the child continue. Be a quiet scribe. One sentence can be enough: "I love you. I miss you."

4. When you are aware of the emotion fueling a behavior, help the child name it: fear, anger, sadness, even guilt. We feel all of these at different times. Talk about what might help when feeling this way. Share what you do.

5. A child might like a special keepsake that helps them feel close and connected to their loved one. When my grandmother died, my father gave me her favorite shawl.

6. Be honest if the child comes to you with questions. Respect their ability to understand, to want to know, and their readiness to talk. Many times we simply need to answer with, "I don't know … what do you think?"

Throughout, be gentle with yourself. You are giving your child the words and the permission to express their feelings. Not an easy task when you are also grieving.